CAN DO
Sticks and Stones

Books in the series:

 Familiar Things
by Sally Thomas

 Eco–Ventures
by Hannah Sugar, Kids' Clubs Network

 Serious Fun: Games for 4–9s
by Phill Burton, Dynamix

 Whatever the Weather
by Jane Gallagher

 Cool Creations
by Mary Allanson, Kids' Clubs Network

 Serious Fun: Games for 10–14s
by Phill Burton, Dynamix

 Sticks and Stones
by Sharon Crockett

Series Foreword

Children and young people of all ages should be able to initiate and develop their own play. Adult involvement should be based on careful observation, appropriate consultation and response to what the children need in terms of their development at this time and in this place.

Play is freely chosen personally directed behaviour motivated from within. Adults can create the best possible conditions for play: the time, space, materials, safety and support for children to develop the skills and understanding they need to extend the possibilities of their play. The degree to which the children and young people are able to make any activity their own will determine its success as a play opportunity rather than simply 'entertainment', a means of 'keeping them busy' or producing 'something to take home to parents'.

Many of the ideas in these books are not new. Indeed play games and creative activities are passed on across many generations and between different cultures across the world, constantly being adapted and changed to suit a new time, a new group of children, a new environment.

We have acknowledged sources and sought permission wherever it has been possible to do so. We hope, and indeed anticipate, that the ideas in these books will be adapted and developed further by those that use them and would be very interested to hear your comments, thoughts, ideas and suggestions.
www.thomsonlearning.co.uk/childcare

Annie Davy

CAN DO
Sticks and Stones

By **Sharon Crockett**

Series Editor: **Annie Davy**

THOMSON

Australia • Canada • Mexico • Singapore • Spain • United Kingdom • United States

Sticks and Stones

Copyright © Sharon Crockett 2002

The Thomson logo is a registered trademark used herein under licence.

For more information, contact Thomson, High Holborn House, 50–51 Bedford Row, London, WC1R 4LR or visit us on the World Wide Web at: http://www.thomsonlearning.co.uk

British Library Cataloguing-in-Publication Data
A catalogue record for this book is available from the British Library

ISBN 1-86152-840-X

First edition 2002

Typeset by Bottle & Co., Banbury, UK

Printed in Croatia by Zrinski

Text design by Bottle & Co.

Contents

Series Introduction   vi-vii

Introduction   viii

Acknowledgements   viii

Craft

Dragon Eyes	1
Dreamcatchers	4
Mobiles	7
Pet Rocks	9
Stick Puppets	12
Stone and Chalk Carving	14
Stone Painting	16

Games

A Game for One	19
Jackstones	21
Mancala	24
Nine Men's Morris	27
Pick-up Sticks	30
Pulijudam—Tigers and Lambs	32
Sixteen Skippers	35

Out and About

Feed the Birds	38
Growing Beans	41
Sculptures using Interesting Wooden Shapes	45
Search and Rescue	49
Trail Laying	51
Travelling Sticks	53

Skills for Life

Building Dens	56
Fire Building	60
Cooking with Sticks	64
Sky Hooks	67
Whittling Sticks	71

Series Introduction

The CAN DO series is an intensely practical resource for children who attend childcare settings, drop in centres or playsettings out of school, and for those of you who work with them in these settings. Anyone working with children, whether as a trainee, an experienced manager or as a volunteer will sometimes get tired, feel jaded or simply seek new inspiration. Whether you are a childminder, a playworker, a family centre worker or a day nursery assistant or manager, you will find a rich source of ideas for children of all ages in the CAN DO series. In these books you will find practical answers to the difficult 'CAN DO' questions which are often asked of adults working with children:

- Child coming in from school, 'What can I do today?'
- Parent visiting a childminder: 'What exactly can the children do here?'
- Playworker or Childcare worker at a team meeting: 'What can we do to extend the range of play provision here?'

The series is structured towards 3 different age ranges 0–3, 4–9 and 10–14, but many of the books will be used successfully by or with older or younger children. The books are written by authors with a wide range of experience in working with children and young people, and who have a thorough understanding of the value of play and the possibilities and constraints of work in childcare and play settings.

Each activity is introduced with a 'why we like it' section, which explains why children and adults who work with children have found this to be something that they enjoyed, or that has enhanced their play provision. Many of the activities also have 'Snapshots' and 'Spotlight' boxes which expand on the possibilities as developed by children, or an approach you can take in working with children. These sections are intended to help you reflect on your work and quality of what is provided.

The ideas in this series are intended to be playful, inclusive and affordable. They are not based on any prescribed curriculum, but they could be used to enrich and develop almost any setting in which children play and learn. They do not rely on expensive toys and equipment; they are environmentally friendly and are peppered with practical tips and health and safety checkpoints.

Language used in the book

YOU (the reader): The books are addressed to children and the adults who work with them together. Older children will be able to use the books themselves or with a little co-operation from adults. There are some activities where adult supervision or assistance will be required (in developing and supervising safe working with tools for example) and this is highlighted where relevant.

SETTING: We have used the term 'setting' rather than club, scheme, centre, etc. as the generic term to describe the range of contexts for childcare and playwork including childminders' homes. The 'Snapshots' draw on a range of different settings to illustrate the development of some of the activities in practice.

PLAYLEADER: This term is predominantly used in the 4–9 and 10–14 series, as this is the most familiar generic term that covers adults working with these age groups in out of school settings.

Sticks and Stones

Finding activities for the 10–14 age group in an out of school setting can be challenging for the adult workers, since, by this stage, young people may not be prepared to play for the sake of it. They need activities, which are stimulating and fun, yet do not reflect or mirror school work. The object of this book is to provide tried and tested ideas that can be adapted to your own setting and environment without purchasing lots of expensive materials and equipment.

Introduction

Why Sticks and Stones? These materials have been used by peoples of the world, for survival and entertainment, for as long as there has been human development. They are readily available and endlessly versatile and adaptable to different cultures and environments. This book contains 26 crafts, games and other activities using sticks and stones in an imaginative and creative way. Some of them can be done in large groups, others in pairs or alone. Some are cooperative; others more competitive, thus providing a balance reflecting young people's various needs and interests.

The activities, as a whole, reflect a variety of cultural backgrounds. This is important because it mirrors and celebrates the cultural diversity, which makes our society so unique and exciting. It also reflects the history and origins of many of the games played by our young people today. A game or activity that may well have started in China or India thousands of years ago, can today often be found in a slightly different form in other parts of the world.

Many of the ideas in this book are ideally suited to outdoor play. It is especially important today to not forget how to have fun outside away from the TV and computer or electronic games. Less familiar activities

such as building a den or experimenting with growing things may encounter some peer resistance at first, but persevere, as the rewards are great. There is nothing better than cooking food over an open fire or building a structure that will be used or admired over and over again.

The opportunity to use tools in a safe and appropriate manner are really important at a time when more traditional craft activities are being squeezed out of the school curriculum. Many of the ideas in this book involve woodwork and other practical skills. Although, there are health and safety implications for many of the projects, do not allow this to put you off as with careful planning and supervision, sharp tools need not be regarded as dangerous. By trying out some of these activities you will build up your tool kit, create valuable play equipment and exciting new spaces.

The following ideas will provide new and challenging experiences for many young people and open the way to further exploration of related activities. These could provide the basis for your setting's own collection of stimulating projects, which could inspire other groups around you. Above all, it is hoped you will have many hours of fun.

Acknowledgements for *Sticks and Stones*

I would like to thank the following people for their time, ideas, help and support—Andy Little, Rachel Hills, George Lowe, Bill Harrison, Helen Osborn, Noah Derrington, Stuart Bell, Chris Hills, Niall Derrington, Dave Wyatt and of course the editor of the Can Do series Annie Davy.

Dragon Eyes

Why we like it

This is an activity that doesn't need expensive materials and is a good introduction into thinking and talking about other cultures. It is good for developing fine motor skills, as it involves simple and repetitive movements. It also promotes concentration on the task in hand. Everyone ends up making something that looks wonderful.

Fig.1

What you might need

Different coloured balls of wool

For each dragon eye: two sticks cut to about 20–24 cm long, diameter can be anything from 3–6 cm

Secateurs (only allow responsible people to use)

Scissors.

How many can do it

5 or 6.

Where you can do it

This can be done inside or out—depending on the weather!

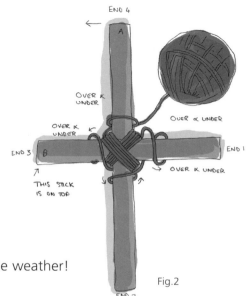

Fig.2

How you can do it

1. In one hand, hold the sticks together, with stick B on top of stick A, to make the shape of a cross. Using your other hand wrap the wool tightly tound the centre of the sticks using cross lashing (see Fig.1), until it is secure. No knots are necessary.

2. Using the same ball of wool, start to form the dragon's eye. With one hand constantly turning the cross in an anti-clockwise direction, the other hand winds the wool firmly around each stick—over end 1, under end 1; under end 2, over end 2; over end 3, under end 3; under end 4, over stick 4 (see Fig.2). Continue this sequence, making sure that as you work your way out from the centre, each strand of wool fits snugly next to the last (Fig.2) Don't rush this process as mistakes are easily made.

3. When you want to change colour, cut the wool you are using, leaving a 5 cm 'tail' (see fig 3). Choose another colour. Don't tie a knot, just wrap it twice over the tail so the first colour can't escape. Start the over and under sequence again, still working in an anti-clockwise direction as before. Don't worry about the tied-in 'sticking-out' tails, as these will be cut off at the end (see Fig.4).

4. Carefully work your way to the end of the sticks, changing colour as often as you like. By now you will have several bands of diamond shaped colours.

5. To finish, cut approximately a 7 cm tail and tie a double knot around the last over or under strand to hold the wool securely.

6. Cut off the left over tails.

7. To hang your dragon's eye up, cut a piece of wool approximately 40 cm long and tie a single knot at the end of one of the sticks. Wrap it round the stick 3 times and secure it with a double knot. Then knot the 2 ends together to form a loop.

8. Dragon's eyes look lovely hung up almost anywhere but try making smaller ones at Christmas to hang on the tree.

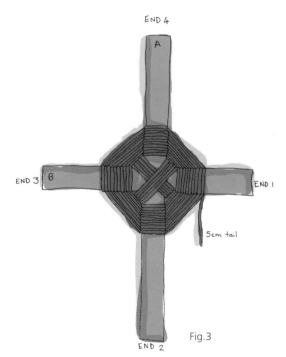

Fig.3

Safety Check

Make sure the ends of the sticks are cut straight to prevent people being poked in the eye accidentally!

Snapshot

A small group of us sat under a tree making dragon eyes. At first a fair amount of supervision was needed as lots of questions were being asked and mistakes being made. However no one got frustrated and as soon as the technique was mastered a kind of purposeful silence descended amongst us, only interrupted by someone asking another to pass the scissors, etc. Everyone was delighted with their finished dragon eye, especially Chloe who, most days, rushed around playing more physical games and for whom sitting down for such a long period of time was unusual. We hung them from an empty curtain rail and they made a lovely display.

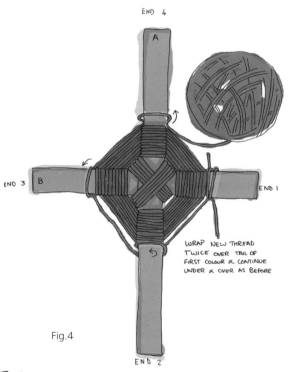

END 4
A
END 3 B
END 1
WRAP NEW THREAD TWICE OVER TAIL OF FIRST COLOUR & CONTINUE UNDER & OVER AS BEFORE
Fig.4
END 2

Useful Tips

Balls of wool can often be picked up at jumble sales for next to nothing or you can unravel old jumpers!

Willow branches (withes) are ideal but any straight twigs can be used. Look out for people trimming their hedge.

If using hedge trimmings, it's a good idea to prepare the wood at home by cutting it to size and cutting off all the knobbly bits with secateurs to avoid snagging the wool.

Don't worry if you make a mistake in the 'under–over sequence', it's easy to unwind and start again.

What Next?

A variation of this activity can be achieved by initially binding the sticks together in an 'X' position as this creates a different wool pattern.

Feathers and beads can be tied to the finished Dragon Eye to create a more decorative effect.

Spotlight

Dragon Eyes take their origin from the Indians of north-west Mexico who called them God's Eyes. They believe that god is everywhere in nature and that the four points of the cross represent earth, water, fire and air. When making the God's Eyes, the Huichol Indians say a prayer in the hope that nature will watch over them.

Dreamcatchers

Why we like this activity

Most people really enjoy making dreamcatchers. They like the legend and the magic of creating something so special. It offers opportunities to learn a new skill and time to sit quietly and concentrate.

What you might need

Newly cut or soaked willow or hazel branches (withes) approximately 120 cm long and $\frac{1}{2}$ cm thick (which will make a circle of about 25 cm diameter)

Selection of thin wool and strong cotton yarn (not dressmaking cotton)

Selection of feathers (which you have collected yourselves if possible)

Scissors

Measuring tape

Selection of beads.

Useful Tips

Willow withes are strong flexible branches from a willow tree. They are often used for binding and basket-making.

How many can do it

This is definitely a small group activity. No more than 5–6 at a time.

Where you can do it

This is a very relaxing, calming activity so try to find a quiet spot away from hustle and bustle. Ideally on a warm day, if you have the facilities, sit in the open air, under a tree.

Spotlight

American Indians were the first people to make dreamcatchers and hang them over their beds in order to sift good and bad dreams. They were traditionally made of willow boughs using sinew for the web and decorated with sage. Now, however they have developed into something of an art form and can be found in the shops made of a wide variety of materials.

This activity will show you just one of the many ways to make a dreamcatcher and once you have grasped the fundamental techniques you will be able to experiment with different sizes and materials to incorporate your own ideas.

How you can do it

Fig.1

1. Carefully bend the willow into a circle and twist the ends around to the required diameter (see Fig.1). This will secure the frame.

2. Cut a 6 m length of yarn and wind it into a small ball around your fingers.

3. Knot one end of the yarn to the circle and wrap it around several times to hide the knot.

Fig.2

4. Working in a clockwise direction, start to make the spider's web by making 9 half-hitch knots, taking the yarn around the willow then through the loop, approximately 3 to 4 cm apart from each other (see Fig.2). Tie the knots loosely so that you can adjust the spacing at the end of your first circle. When you are happy that the knots are where you want them, pull the yarn tight (Fig.3). As you work your way round, keep the yarn tight to create the 'diamond' like shapes (see Fig.3).
Note: Fig.3 and Fig.4 show the yarn before it is pulled tight, so that you can see the knotting pattern.

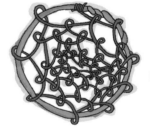

Fig.3

5. Carry on weaving in the same way until you have a small hole left in the middle. Keep turning the circle as you work and periodically make sure the frame is still as round as possible. As the hole in the middle gets smaller, the web shapes also get smaller, so tying the knots becomes very fiddly (see Fig.4)—be patient and don't rush!

Fig.4

6. When you are happy that the hole is small enough, tie off the yarn using a couple of half hitches. Do not cut the yarn but leave it hanging below the dreamcatcher and securely attach a feather.

7. Lastly, tie a loop at the top of the dreamcatcher so you can hang it up (see Fig.5). Sweet dreams!

Fig.5

Safety Check

Make sure that the scissors are used appropriately.

What next?

Personalise your dreamcatcher by weaving in small personal items or pieces of bark, leaves, etc.

Beads of all shapes and colours can be spun into the web the second time around as long as the knotting technique has been mastered.

Dreamcatchers and Dragon's eyes would look really lovely together hung in benders and tipis (see page 56) or hanging from a Sky hook (see page 67). If you have been inspired by making dreamcatchers and the legend why not look at *http://elfwood.lysator.liu.se/loth/p/u/puimun/dreamcatchers.ipg.html* to see two beautiful pictures based on dreamcatchers by the artist Stephanie Pui-Mun-Law. Perhaps you too could paint or draw some wonderful dream pictures or make a dreamcatcher for a younger child who gets nightmares. One legend has it that as dreams are sent to you, the good dreams find their way through the hole in the middle of the web and float down the feather(s) to the person sleeping. The bad are caught in the web where the morning sun makes them perish at first light. There are several different legends attached to dreamcatchers, see below, so you can choose which one you like best.

Useful Tips

Try this activity out at home first so that you can demonstrate confidently!

'Hairy wool' such as mohair is pretty but difficult to use—don't use it the first time you try the activity.

Do demonstrate the activity—especially the knots.

Stagger the starting point of each individual.

Spotlight—Another Legend

A long time ago, an old spiritual leader had a vision. He saw Iktomi, the teacher of wisdom, in the shape of a spider. Iktomi picked up his willow hoop which was covered in beads and feathers and began to spin a web. As he span he began to speak about the cycle of life—from birth to death—and the web of good and bad forces that could influence one's life. When he had finished, there was a perfect circle with a hole in the middle. He handed it back to the leader explaining that the leader's people should use the web to read their ideas, dreams and visions and thereby achieve their ambitions. The web would catch their positive ideas whilst the negative ones would pass through the hole. Since then many people have hung a dreamcatcher over their bed in order for the web to catch the good dreams and let fly through the hole and away from their lives, the bad.

Mobiles

Why we like it

Mobiles are fun and simple to make. They can be made any size you like, individually or in groups, reflect a theme or tell a story (as do travelling sticks on page 53). They make great displays, which can be changed to reflect the seasons or different cultural festivals. In addition they make good presents, especially for a younger brother or sister.

What you might need

Sticks or garden canes

Driftwood, dead heather or interestingly shaped sticks

Collected items such as feathers, pebbles, shells, leaves, conkers, acorns, etc

Strong thread or wool, or nylon thread (this is best because it is strong, waterproof and 'invisible')

Varnish

Scissors

Hand drill and small wood bit

Workbench with vice

Safety goggles.

How many can do it

Groups of 8–10.

Where you can do it

Indoors or out.

Safety Check

Make sure wood is held securely in the vice before starting to drill and that no one is rushing around in that area.

White spirit can be harmful if used incorrectly. Wear rubber gloves and if any should accidentally splash on your skin, wash it off immediately using soap and water.

Remember to wear safety goggles when drilling.

Spotlight

Mobiles are easy to create and, because they have to hang above head height, they encourage a look at your ceiling or the sky. They can be hung inside or out, be soundless or created to make a tuneful noise, be designed to show wind direction or just look pretty. With a bit of thought, you can add texture, lights, reflection and colour to make a mobile with a difference, suited to individuals needs.

How you can do it

Method 1

1. Take an interesting shaped stick or piece of driftwood and secure it firmly in a vice.

2. Decide how many holes you wish to drill in it and mark their positions with a pencil.

3. Now carefully drill the holes all the way through the wood in each of the positions marked.

4. Put a long piece of thread through each of the holes and tie it off securely. Make sure that the thread is a lot longer than the finished required length as you will be using it to wrap around, or tie in, hanging items.

5. Now work your way down each thread tying in or wrapping around items as you go. Small holes can be made in shells or conkers using the drill. This needs to be done slowly and gently to prevent them from breaking.

6. Cut off any unused thread at the bottom of each string before varnishing each item for a glossy finish.

Method 2

1. Take two sticks and lash them together in a cross shape.

2. Attach one of your four strings (as above) to the end of each stick.

3. Attach a hanging string, to the centre of the cross and adjust the balance by moving the central lashing and the hanging strings backwards and forwards. Once you are happy that the mobile is balanced, put a blob of glue on the lashing and the hanging strings to fix them permanently in place.

4. Hang outside or inside in an area where people will not bump their head on the mobile.

Snapshot

Leon and Zara's mother recently had a new baby and they wanted to make something for him. After a great deal of discussion, they decided on a mobile. From a local park, they collected sticks and pinecones, which were lying, scattered about on the ground. They strung them up on the cross structure and then painted each cone in a bright colour so that they would catch the baby's attention as he lay in his cot. They were both really pleased with the finished effect.

Useful Tips

It is easier to make the mobiles on a table and then hang up at the end, rather than hang them before completing each string.

If you don't want to attach a central string by wrapping it round the stick (as in Method 1) you might screw in a small hook instead.

Always clean varnish brushes immediately after use, using white spirit in a small pot.

What next?

Why not try making even more complex mobiles by hanging additional layers of sticks and threads off the initial cross structure. Balancing can be tricky at times but with a little time and perseverance, you will make it work.

Pet Rocks

Why we like it

This is a chance for everyone to use their imagination and be as creative as they like. Pet Rocks are fun to create and make lovely presents or keepsakes.

What you might need

Pebbles

Tile cement

Enamel or Acrylic paint

Varnish (water-based if possible)

White spirit

Old newspaper

Washing up liquid

Thin paint brushes

Disposable plastic gloves

Scrubbing brushes or old toothbrushes

Spatulas

Measuring jug

Varnishing brush

Hairdryer (optional).

How many can do it

Groups of up to 8.

Where you can do it

Inside or out but this is a good wet weather indoor activity, as long as there is somewhere to dry wet paint.

How you can do it

1. It is a good idea to have some pictures or previously made examples of pet rocks to show in order to stimulate ideas of creatures or figures that could be made. Maybe ideas will come from a story or book which someone has read recently.

2. Choose your stones and talk about the figures you are going to make—it may be a clown, dragon or animal of some sort!

3. Scrub the stones in buckets of water and washing up liquid.

4. Leave to dry or use a hairdryer.

5. Mix up the tiling cement—just follow the instructions on the packet but be precise with the proportions.

6. Wearing rubber gloves and using a spatula or stick, fix stones together in the formation required.

7. Leave to dry— this may take up to 24 hours.

8. Using paint, create your creature or figure. Think about colours and brush sizes, for example, a small smiley mouth requires a very thin brush.

9. When the paint is dry, test a very small area with varnish to check that the paint doesn't smudge. If fine, coat with several layers of varnish to withstand weather, time and polishing.

10. Give your pet rock a name and a home!

Spotlight

Many people, lucky enough to live by the sea, use the pebbles they find on the beach to create and make things with. However, it is not just those who live by the sea who use the natural and sometimes discarded manufactured items around them. In many parts of the world, children and young people make play items or activities from the things they find around them. Tin cans are cut open and bashed flat to make push along trucks, dice are made from discarded blocks of wood and pebbles are painted to depict special events such as a local band or gathering. The following activity follows a long history of using what was available before plastic and toyshops cornered the market and perhaps took some of the imagination out of play.

Safety Check

Tile cement contains chemicals, which could harm skin and eyes. Be careful to wear gloves, not touch your eyes and wash your hands thoroughly.

When cleaning brushes in white spirit, wear rubber gloves and be careful not to splash your eyes.

Useful Tips

Enamel and acrylic paints are comparatively expensive so limit brush sizes and only use one brush per colour. It could be an expensive disaster if the colours get mixed.

Plan this activity over a number of sessions, because an immediate result is not possible. It's a good activity for a group that meets once a week or over the course of a whole week.

A cheap bag of mixed pebbles can be bought from a DIY store.

Enamel paint brushes should be cleaned in white spirit, acrylic paint brushes in water.

Snapshot

A group of eleven year old boys decided to make two five a side football teams. They made up the figures, designed the strips and gave the teams names. When they had finished, they drew out a pitch on a large sheet of paper, made goals from sticks and played a match using a ping-pong ball and very loud commentary. They later decided to make a referee as well!

What next?

Instead of everybody creating their own figures, why not make this into a group activity with members making a figure connected to a theme or story.

Stick Puppets

Why we like it

This is a good winter activity that is fun, creative and stimulates the imagination.

What you might need

Thin white card
Two pin brass paper fasteners
Masking tape
Felt pens and pencils
Thin garden sticks about
30–40 cm long
Cooking oil
Scissors
Hole punch
Clip on lamp with 100w. bulb.

How many can do it

As many as you have materials for, split into small groups.

Where you can do it

Indoors on a table.

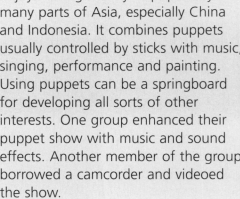

Spotlight

Shadow puppetry is a folk art which enjoys a long history of popularity in many parts of Asia, especially China and Indonesia. It combines puppets usually controlled by sticks with music, singing, performance and painting. Using puppets can be a springboard for developing all sorts of other interests. One group enhanced their puppet show with music and sound effects. Another member of the group borrowed a camcorder and videoed the show.

Useful Tips

Make the figures big and bold as these will make more effective shadow puppets.

Keep the groups small to start with otherwise they will all be tripping over each other behind the screen.

Do allow some time for rehearsal—your puppet show will be much more satisfying and professional.

How you can do it

1. Decide in your groups what your puppet show is going to be about. Are you going to write your own story or act out an old favourite? Now decide on how many puppets you need and who or what they are.

2. Work out how many pieces your puppet needs, for example, arms, legs, body, etc. and draw each piece separately onto the card, slightly larger than necessary to allow for a joining overlap.

3. Cut out the pieces and make holes where they join.

4. Decorate both sides with coloured pencils, felt pens or crayons and rub cooking oil on the front of the pieces in order to make your puppet translucent.

5. Join the pieces together making sure that the smooth heads of the fasteners are on the front of your figure.

6. Decide which pieces you are going to attach sticks to and fix them on the back with masking tape.

7. Now rig up your sheet screen and the lamp. The lamp needs to be behind the screen and up higher than where your puppets will be performing.

8. Turn the lights off and let the show begin!

Safety Check

Make sure the lamp is securely fixed and that its wire is not near the performance area.

Snapshot

One group at a local holiday play scheme, became very enthusiastic about this activity and decided to make puppets from traditional stories. As they became more experienced, the puppets, became more elaborate with lots of additional features. At the end of the holiday, they asked if they could do a performance at a local nursery. It was so well received by the children and their carers, that they were duly invited to appear at a number of other creches and playgroups in the area. It was wonderful to watch their confidence grow as they completed yet another successful performance.

What next?

Instead of using felt pens, try inks and dyes for different colour effects. Also try making other types of puppets using wooden spoons and sticks as bodies with paper bag, plastic bottle or papier-mache heads.

Stone and Chalk Carving

Why we like it

This is a good activity to introduce the principles of how to use tools correctly so that the user and those around remain safe and unharmed. It can be used as a way into talking about safe working spaces, the use and care of tools and the importance of following instructions.

What you might need

Blocks of soft stone, such as, sandstone or a composite building block, cut roughly 15 cm square

Protective dust masks and old clothes

A groundsheet to collect dust and chippings

A selection of different sized metal files and rasps

Safety goggles.

Useful Tips

Composite building blocks can be purchased from most building merchants and landscape walling companies, types of stone vary across the country. If you are lucky to live near a quarry, small off-cuts may given freely.

Useful Tips

If you have access to good quality chisels and small picks and an adult who is confident in teaching and supervising the correct use of these tools, more sophisticated carvings can be achieved.

How many can do it

As many as you have got materials and equipment for and feel comfortable supervising.

Where you can do it

This really is an outdoor activity as a lot of dust is created.

How you can do it

1. Think of a simple shape you would like to make; a face, an animal, etc.

2. Draw the design onto one side of the block.

3. Now keeping the block steady between your knees, begin to shape it by rubbing the block using the different sized files. If using the clipping tools do not hold the block between your knees.

4. When you are happy with your shape, leave it in its natural state or decorate it.

Spotlight

Boys sometimes avoid creative activities preferring more active running or ball games, so it's important to find some that will immediately appeal. Crafts can improve fine motor skills, concentration and an eye for fine detail—important learning skills for life. Finding one that is enjoyable and fun will often open the door to other craft activities. Likewise, girls will often avoid more physical games, so, in this case, it is important to find one that appeals to the girls in your setting and once you've found it, others can gradually be introduced.

Useful Tips

Don't be too ambitious on your first attempt!

Plan this activity to perhaps last an hour a day over a number of sessions.

Safety Check

This activity may not be suitable for asthma sufferers.

It's best to wear trousers to avoid grazed knees.

If you are using chipping tools make sure everyone is wearing safety goggles.

Use the file in a rubbing rather than stabbing manner.

Ensure tools are used in a safe and appropriate manner.

Snapshot

I watched my son amongst a group of young people, absorbed for hours in this activity. At the end of the session, he proudly presented me with his rock. 'Here you go mum. It's a cliff for your seagull!' And so it is.

 ## What next?

Why not invite a local sculptor in to demonstrate a range of carving techniques.

Think about other materials to carve, such as wood, or other ways to sculpt such as using clay or moulds with Plaster of Paris.

Stone Painting—Canal Boat Style

Why we like it

This is a good rainy day activity and the stones can be used to decorate a garden area or water feature or simply as a good old-fashioned paperweight. Of course you can paint anything you like but this example suggests the traditional colours and designs of barge painting, as the finished result is beautifully decorative.

What you might need

Large round pebbles

Enamel paint—black, red, white, blue and yellow

Kitchen roll

White spirit

White chalk

Pictures of traditional canal barge paintings

Small pots or pallets

Brushes: a thick one for the base coat, a No.1 and a No.7.

How many can do it

A group of 4 or 5 depending on how many brushes you have.

Where you can do it

On a table either inside or out.

Useful Tips

It's really important to leave the different colours to dry between stages otherwise you will end up with a mess! So plan to do this activity over a number of days.

Make sure the brushes are cleaned using white spirit and kitchen towel between colours.

Brush strokes should always run from top to bottom—it is much more difficult to paint the other way round.

Do try this out at home first so that you can demonstrate the different stages confidently—although it is not as complicated as it sounds.

If you make a mistake, don't worry; just wipe it off with kitchen roll and white spirit.

Make sure you wear on old shirt or painting apron, as enamel paint is impossible to get off your clothes.

With very young children, it is advisable to use poster paint and varnish the stones afterwards.

How you can do it

1. Paint all your stones black (it's not necessary to do the bottoms) and leave to dry.

2. Chalk three circles in a triangular pattern on the centre of your stone (see Fig.1)

Fig.1

3. Using the No.7 brush and the colour red, paint a rose in each of the circles. The rose is made by painting two fat petals on each side of the circle. The brush strokes start at the top of the circle and finish at the bottom. Across the top of the circle, using the tip of the brush, paint four or five small petals, as in Fig.2.

Fig.2

4. Mix up a dark green on the pallet by using some blue and a little yellow and paint leaves round your roses. The simplest way to do this is to use the No.7 brush and make two fat brush strokes for the outer edges of the leaf and one to fill in the centre (see Fig.3).

WHITE LINES

Fig.4

5. Using the No.1 brush and the colour white, paint four or five thin lines on top of the rose from top to bottom as in Fig.4.

Fig.3

6. Mix up a paler green by adding more yellow into the dark green and paint veins onto the leaves using the No.1 brush again (see Fig.5).

Fig.5

7. Using the tip of the No. 1 brush and the colour blue, paint a few small blue dots randomly around the roses and leaves. Round each blue dot paint a ring of small white dots using the No. 1 brush. In the centre of each blue dot paint a small yellow dot (see Fig.6)

SMALL FLOWERS

Fig.6

Snapshot

In the children's area at a festival, five children from the same family worked together with the eldest helping the younger ones. Although working from the same basic design each child produced a uniquely different stone. When the stones had dried, the children placed their finished stones together in a herb garden and later in the evening came back with lighted candles and a note that read, 'Remember our grandpa who died last year. We hope you are somewhere happy.'

Spotlight

This style of painting has its origins in the Victorian era when many families moved onto the canals to find work. In order to make their boats more homely; people began painting them and the objects around them. The rose was a particularly popular design because in parts of the country the canals were lined with common dog roses.

Safety Check

If you spill white spirit on your skin, wash it off immediately.

What next?

Once you have mastered the painting technique, try painting old metal objects such as trays, kettles, baked bean and biscuit tins, mugs, etc.

If you would like to learn more about narrow boat painting, try to get hold of *Paint Roses & Castles* by Anne Young, published by David & Charles,1992. ISBN: 0-71539-940-3

A Game for One

Why we like it

Although on the surface, it appears very simple, this puzzle requires concentration and a fair amount of thought. After playing once or twice, strategies are devised and refined.

What you might need

A 25 cm x 25 cm x 18 mm piece of plywood

A 150 cm length of 6 mm dowelling

Sandpaper

Masking tape

Emulsion paint and varnish

Brushes

White spirit

Tape measure, ruler and tri-square

Saw

G-Clamps

Hand drill and 6.5 mm wood drill bit

Safety goggles.

How many can do it

Making the game can be done in pairs but playing it is strictly a one-person affair.

Where you can do it

Inside or outside, depending on the weather.

Spotlight

There are times when everyone wants to be alone—to sit and think, get away from others, walk, read or play a game by themselves. Time spent away from other people should not be seen as being negative since it can often be a rewarding and growing experience. At times of friction, some people need to be encouraged to sit on their own and this game is ideal for quiet contemplation.

Safety Check

Use all tools in an appropriate and safe manner.

Wear rubber gloves when washing out varnish brushes.

Wear safety goggles when drilling.

How you can do it

1. Mark out a 25 cm square on the plywood. Clamp to workbench using G-clamps and cut accurately.

2. Sand round the edges with the sandpaper until smooth.

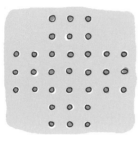

3. Now using a ruler mark out the position of the holes with a pencil (softly). Any lines you draw will be rubbed away later.

4. Again clamp the board to the workbench and start to drill holes in the positions you have marked. Drill holes to a depth of 9 mm. To do this accurately, measure 9 mm from the tip of the drill bit and mark with masking tape. Stop drilling on every hole when the drill bit reaches this depth.

5. Remove saw dust from each of the holes and carefully sand the edges.

6. Using the doweling cut the 32 pegs. Mark out 40 mm lengths of dowelling and cut one at a time — measuring each one accurately as you go.

7. Sand and paint, decorate or varnish the pieces and board if you like.

How you can play the game

1. Place a peg in each hole apart from the centre.
2. Start by jumping one of the pegs horizontally or vertically into the centre.
3. Remove the peg you have jumped over.
4. Repeat until you have only one peg left.

 ### What next?
Make the game more difficult by aiming to finish with the last peg in the centre hole.

Snapshot
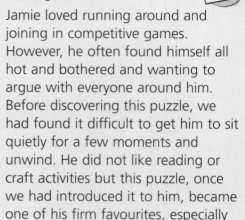

Jamie loved running around and joining in competitive games. However, he often found himself all hot and bothered and wanting to argue with everyone around him. Before discovering this puzzle, we had found it difficult to get him to sit quietly for a few moments and unwind. He did not like reading or craft activities but this puzzle, once we had introduced it to him, became one of his firm favourites, especially after he had made his own. He even enjoyed showing others how to play.

Useful Tips

When sanding, wrap the sandpaper round a block of wood as this gives you an easier surface to hold onto.

After marking the depth of the drill bit, test on an off-cut, not only for depth but also for width, that is, does the dowelling fit snugly?

When drilling make sure the drill is held upright and that only the item in question has holes made in it.

Before drilling the holes, draw soft pencil lines on the board and measure the position of the holes accurately.

For accurate drilling, make a small indent at the centre of the cross with a nail or a bradawl.

For straight drilling, place a large tri-square against the board to use as a visual guide.

Two coats of varnish will make the board and pegs last longer.

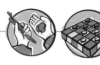

Jackstones

Why we like it

Originally from Pakistan, this version of Jackstones is fantastically simple and fun to make and play. It's an especially good game to know as a 'fill in' when out and about as the board can be drawn into the earth using a stick and pebbles collected from round about.

What you might need

Five small pebbles (the Jackstones)

One larger pebble per player (the counter)

Large sheet of cardboard

Different coloured large marker pens

Ruler

Something to draw a large circle round, for example, a large plate.

How many can do it

In groups of 4.

Where you can do it

Inside or out.

Spotlight

'Jacks' was a popular game in the past, regularly found on school playgrounds. It was played using 3-dimensional metal crosses (Jacks) and the object of the game was to bounce a small ball with one hand and pick up a certain number of Jacks with the other.

How you can do it

1. Decorate each of the larger pebbles.

2. Draw a large circle on the cardboard and a cross inside the circle, effectively dividing the circle into four equal parts.

3. Using the ruler, divide each of the four lines into ten equal parts, as shown.

4. Decorate the board, if you like.

How you can play the game

1. Each player places his or her counter at the point where a line meets the edge of the circle.

2. To decide who starts, each player takes a turn at tossing all five Jackstones in the air and catching them on the back of both hands. The person who catches the most begins the game.

3. Each player takes it in turns to toss and catch the Jackstones on the back of their hands. If no stones are caught, the Jackstones are passed to the next player; if one stone is caught then the counter is advanced one mark towards the centre; if two, two marks; if three, the player's turn ends and the stones are passed on; if four, four marks towards the centre are moved and if five, the player must attempt to toss the stones from the back of the hands and catch them in the palm of their hands. If all five are caught then the counter is moved five marks, if not then the player cannot move their counter.

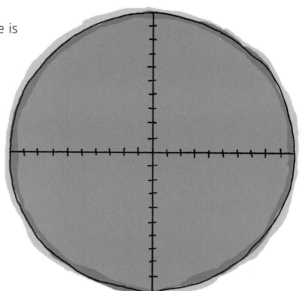

4. The first player to reach the centre is the winner.

Useful Tips

Choose rounded, rather than sharp pebbles as these will be easier to catch and less likely to bounce off the back of your hands.

The board could be drawn in damp sand or with chalk on the pavement.

Don't throw the stones too high as this makes them difficult to catch.

Snapshot

Julie, Fred, Amna and Samantha were four young people who found it very difficult to get along with others. However, this was one game they could play together as it relies on individual effort and not having to depend on others, for example, such as in a team situation. They enjoyed it so much that they each went and found and painted their own set of stones that they often carried around in their pockets.

What next?

To make the game more difficult try tossing and catching using only one hand and then if you are right-handed try using your left hand and vice-versa.

Try playing the game using the same rules but use short sticks instead of stones— as did some North American Indians in the past.

Mancala

Why we like it

The activity involves making your own version of this popular game, which becomes a permanent play resource, and learning to play it with your friends. This involves interaction, strategy building and thinking skills.

What you might need

Three $\frac{1}{2}$ dozen egg boxes per game

Masking tape

Old newspaper

Wallpaper paste

Paint

PVA glue

48 small round stones per game

Scissors

Bucket

Paint and glue brushes

Varnish

Some pictures or materials depicting African designs.

How many can do it

Groups of up to 6, working in pairs.

Where you can do it

Inside or outside depending on the weather.

Spotlight

Mancala, also called Wari, is a game, which is played in parts of West Africa and the Caribbean. It can become highly competitive, depending on the players. However don't let this put you off making and playing the game, as it's great fun and can develop high levels of strategy and skill. Some young people need and relish competition, which is no bad thing when balanced with a good mixture of cooperative games.

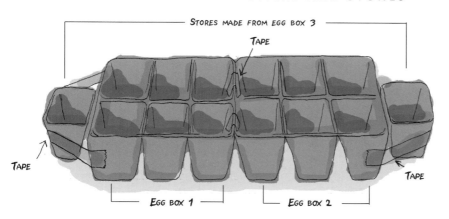

Stores made from egg box 3

Tape

Tape

Tape

Egg box 1

Egg box 2

How you can do it

1. Arrange the egg boxes and tape together.

2. Tear newspaper into thin strips and mix up the wallpaper paste in a bucket.

3. Paint the paste evenly onto the strips and begin layering onto your eggbox base. Make sure that the strips follow the contours of the eggboxes. 4 or 5 layers should be sufficient.

4. When all the newspaper is securely stuck, leave to dry overnight.

5. When the board is dry, begin to decorate it (you could use some of the ideas from the African designs).

6. Leave the paint to dry and then coat with PVA.

7. Now, you are ready to play the game and this is how...

How you can play the game

This game is for two players, sitting on either side of the board.

1. Place four stones in each hole, leaving the two stores (at each end) empty.

2. Player 1 picks up the four stones from any one hole on their side and, moving anti-clockwise, places one stone in each consecutive hole, including their own store, on their right, but not their opponent's store. If your last stone falls in your store, you have another turn. So pick up all the stones from any one hole on your side and repeat, always moving anti-clockwise. When your turn has finished, player 2 takes a turn. Player 2 repeats the same process as above (see page 26).

3. The object of the game is to collect as many pieces as possible in your store. There are two ways of doing this. Either drop them in as explained in 2 or you can take your opponent's pieces by dropping your last stone into an empty hole on your side. You can then collect all your opponent's stones from opposite the hole you last played in and drop them in your store.

4. The game continues until one player has no pieces on his or her side of the board, not including their store. The winner is the person with the most stones on their side of the board including their store.

Snapshot

Tyson and Jasmine enjoyed making this game as much as learning how to play it. They painted their board black and decorated it with red and green patterns. It looked really effective. Although they needed help with the rules, after a few tries they soon got the hang of the game and were then able to teach others in the group how to play. For a week or two Mancala tournaments were set up spontaneously and, although they were highly competitive, the group proved very good at showing each other how to play.

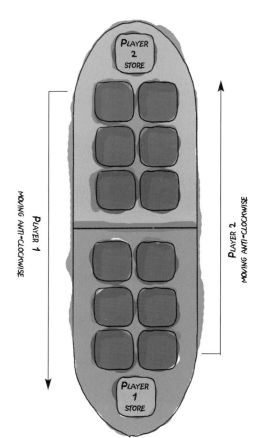

Useful Tips

When making the board, make sure that the strips of newspaper are well coated in glue but not so much that the paper completely disintegrates!

You may decide to paint the stones. If so, give them several coats of varnish for durability.

It's a good idea for one person who knows the game to teach it, through demonstration, to a small group of people until they can play with confidence and then they can teach others.

If lacking a board, try using a tray of damp sand.

Remember you cannot remove stones from either your opponents or your own store.

Safety Check

You should be careful that glue or varnish does not get in anyone's eyes. If, by accident, it does, apply cold water straight away and seek medical help.

Gloves should be worn when using and applying varnish and when washing the brushes.

What Next?

There are many versions of the game and this is only one. Why not investigate others?

Nine Men's Morris

Why we like it

This is a good game to play in pairs and best of all it requires minimal materials. Although it's good to make up a couple of boards, you can just as easily play with wet sand in a tray.

What you might need

Piece of plywood at least 30 cm x 30 cm x 18 mm deep

Sandpaper

Thick felt pen

Varnish

Nine white pebbles and nine brown pebbles

Workbench

Saw

A 30 cm ruler

Varnish brush

Bradawl.

Snapshot

This is a very old game dating back to at least 1400BC. It was very popular with the Romans who brought it to Britain.

How many can do it

Work in pairs. The number of pairs able to participate will vary according to whether the boards are pre-cut.

Where you can do it

Inside or out.

How you can do it

1.   Mark out a piece of plywood 30 cm x 30 cm.

2.   Clamp it securely to the work bench and cut square.

3.   Sand down rough edges.

4.   Using a ruler mark out grid using a pencil at first and when you are happy, go over it with a dark felt pen (Fig.1).

5. Give the board a coat of varnish and leave to dry.

How you can play the game

1.   Taking it in turns, each player places a pebble at any right-angle on the board.

2.   When one player makes a row of three, either horizontally, vertically or diagonally (see Fig.2 for examples) she can take off one of the other's pieces, these cannot be replaced. You cannot remove a pebble from a line of three that has already been made unless there is no other option.

3.   When all the pebbles have been placed on the board, the players take it in turns to move their pieces around the grid to try and make new lines of three. Players can only move their piece to adjacent right-angle.

4.   The winner is the player who has taken all but two of her opponent's pieces or manages to block the pebbles so her opponent can't move.

Fig.1

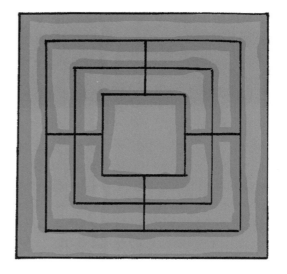

Safety Check

Use all tools appropriately in a supervised area.

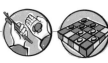

Fig.2

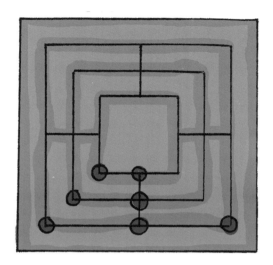

Useful Tips

Unless the group wants to practise their woodwork skills, it is a good idea to pre-cut the boards.

Draw a template on a piece of paper, tape it to the board and, using a bradawl, carefully mark the corners of the grid. Take off the template and join the points together using a ruler.

The key to the game lies in the initial laying of the pieces.

Snapshot

On a trip to the seaside, after swimming and playing ball games, two young people sat down and started playing this game. They collected pebbles from the beach and drew the grid in the sand with their fingers. They played for a while, stopping at the end of each game to discuss strategies. Later, others joined them.

What next?

As mentioned above boards can be simply a tray of wet sand with the grid marked out using a stick.

Alternatively you could roll out a large square of clay or plasticine and mark out the grid using marbles.

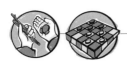

Pick-up Sticks

Why we like it

This is a really simple well-known game that can be quickly taught and requires little supervision. It requires a steady hand and lots of concentration. Making your own Pick-up Sticks extends the activity and enables everyone to personalise his or her game.

What you might need

25 wooden skewers

5 different coloured felt tip pens.

How many can do it

A group of 4 or 5.

Where you can do it

On a level surface inside or out.

Safety Check

Players should try to avoid injuring themselves or others with the skewers. This is highly unlikely but close supervision should be given to the more temperamental players.

Useful Tips

It's a good idea to actually play this game in groups of 5 with one person taking it in turns to be the referee. This way disputes may be avoided.

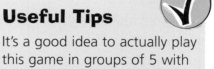

Spotlight

This game was originally played by North American Indians using straws of wheat. It later became popular with settlers who adapted the game by using the sticks around them.

How you can do it

1. Put one skewer aside and divide the remaining 24 into 4 piles.

2. Use a different colour felt tip pen to decorate each pile by drawing on stripes, spots, etc.

3. Completely cover the remaining stick with the 5th colour. This is your pick-up stick.

How you can play the game

1. Each player chooses a colour.

2. One player holds all the sticks upright in one hand, touching the playing surface.

3. On a count of three, the player opens his hand quickly and lets go of the sticks.

4. Taking turns, each player tries to remove one of his coloured sticks from the pile, using the pick-up stick. This can be done by flipping, nudging, rolling or pushing.

5. If the player successfully removes his stick without disturbing the others, he can claim the stick and have another go. However, if another players stick moves, the sticks are left as they are and the next player takes his turn.

6. The game finishes when one player has picked up all their sticks.

Snapshot

Adam and Linsey were completely fascinated by this game, they made several versions of it:

Using drinking straws which were great for tossing in the air

Using more or less players, the person who picked up the most sticks of whatever colour was the winner

Discarding the pick-up stick and just using their fingers

They also made a version of the game with a variety of different types of sticks:

A miniature game using cocktail sticks,

An outdoor game using twigs (the knobblier the better)

Using garden canes to make a large outdoor game.

What next?

To make the game more difficult, allocate points for different coloured sticks, for example, red, 5 points; green 2 points, etc. When all the sticks have been picked up the player with the most points wins.

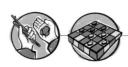

Pulijudam—Tigers and Lambs

Why we like it

This is a good traditional game to play in pairs. The rules are simple and it uses a minimal amount of materials. It makes a good rainy day activity.

What you might need

Piece of plywood at least 30 cm x 30 cm x 18mm deep

Sandpaper

Thick felt pen

Varnish

13 white pebbles and 1 brown pebble (These could be painted from a bag bought from a DIY store)

Workbench

Saw

A 30 cm ruler

Varnish brush

Bradawl

White spirit

G-clamps.

Spotlight

Pulijudam, also called tigers and lambs, is a traditional Indian game dating back thousands of years when tigers were common. An old English variation is called fox and geese. There are lots of different ways of playing it and the one that follows is just one example.

How many can do it

Work in pairs. The number of pairs able to participate will vary according to whether the boards are pre-cut.

Where you can do it

Inside or out.

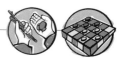

How you can do it

1. Mark out a piece of plywood 30 cm x 30 cm.

2. Clamp securely to work bench and cut square.

3. Sand down rough edges with the sandpaper.

4. Using a ruler, mark out grid using a pencil at first and when you are happy go over it with a dark felt pen (Fig.1).

5. Give the board a coat of varnish and leave to dry.

Fig.1

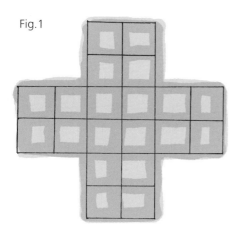

How you can play the game

1. Place the pebbles on the board as shown in Fig.2. One player is the tiger (brown pebble) the other play is the lambs (white pebbles). Turns are taken consecutively.

2. The tiger can move the brown pebble one space forwards, backwards, or sideways along the grid. It can capture a lamb by jumping over it and landing on an empty space. The tiger can capture more than one lamb at a time by making a series of jumps. The captured lambs are removed from the board.

3. The lambs cannot jump over each other or the tiger. They can only move forwards or sideways. The lambs aim to corner the tiger so that it can't move and in that case they win. However if the tiger captures nine lambs, then it is the winner.

Fig.2

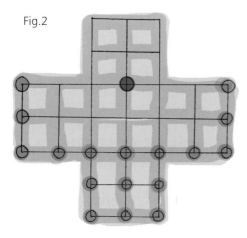

Safety Check

Use all tools appropriately in a supervised area (see Snapshot on page 37).

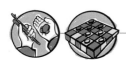

CAN DO

Useful Tips

Unless the group wants to practise their woodwork skills, it is a good idea to pre-cut the boards or buy them cut to size from a timber merchant.

Draw a template on a piece of paper, tape it to the board and using a bradawl, carefully mark the corners of the grid. Take off the template and join the points together using a ruler.

Snapshot

Avril and Catherine, two fairly musical girls, were playing this game one day when they started to also talk about some shows they had recently seen on TV. All of a sudden they cleared the board and started again. The tiger became a producer and the lambs potential popstars.

What next?

Try drawing out different shaped grids on paper and varying the number of tigers and lambs. Perhaps you'll be able to make up a completely new version of this game.

Other variations could include allowing the tigers or lambs or both to move diagonally or forwards. Yet another version could be to place two or more tigers on the board and add a lamb to the grid, for each move a tiger makes, until the agreed number of lambs are on the board.

PAGE 34

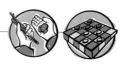

Sixteen Skippers

Why we like it

Making board games provide simple woodworking projects with a finished result that can be used by all time and time again. The best of both worlds—we end up with a permanent play resource, whilst providing a fun and creative play opportunity.

What you might need

A piece of plywood 25 cm x 25 cm x 18 mm deep

A 150 cm dowelling

Sandpaper

Masking tape

Emulsion paint and varnish

Brushes

Permanent pen

Tape measure, ruler and tri-square

Saw

G-clamps

Hand drill and 6.5 mm wood drill bit

White spirit.

How many can do it

In groups of 2.

Where you can do it

Inside.

Useful Tips

When sanding, wrap the sandpaper round a block of wood as this gives you an easier surface to hold onto.

After marking the depth of the drill bit, test on an off-cut, not only for depth but also for width, that is, does the dowelling fit snugly?

When drilling make sure the drill is held upright and that only the item in question has holes made in it.

Two coats of varnish will make the board and pegs last longer.

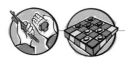

How you can do it

1. Mark out a 50 cm square on the plywood. Clamp to workbench using G-clamps and cut accurately.

2. Sand round the edges until smooth.

3. Now using a ruler mark out the grid with a pencil, as in Fig.1. When you are sure you have got it correct, go over the lines with a dark permanent pen.

Fig.1

4. Again clamp the board to the workbench and start to drill holes at all points where the lines meet. Drill holes to a depth of 9 mm. To do this accurately, measure 9 mm from the tip of the drill bit and mark with masking tape. Stop drilling on every hole when the drill bit reaches this depth.

5. Remove saw dust from each of the holes and sand the edges. Re-apply any parts of the grid with the marker.

6. Now cut the dowelling into 32 pieces. Mark out 40 mm lengths and cut one at a time—measuring each one accurately as you go.

7. Sand and paint or decorate the pieces in two different colours - 16 in one colour and 16 in the other.

8. Varnish the board and pegs and leave to dry.

How you can play the game

1. Each player places their pieces as shown in Fig.2.

2. Each player takes turns to move one hole in any direction (forwards, backwards, sideways, diagonally). The idea is to take your opponent's piece or pieces by jumping over them and landing in an empty hole (as in draughts). That piece is then removed from the game. If you can take a piece, you must, otherwise you forfeit your own piece. You cannot jump over your own pieces.

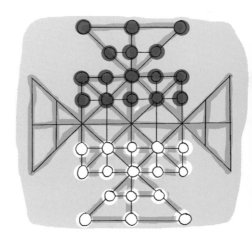

Fig.2

3. The aim of the game is to take all your opponent's pieces.

Spotlight

Woodwork is a great way of learning new skills and how to use potentially dangerous tools sensibly and appropriately. It's an opportunity that should be experienced by all, as it increases confidence and practical abilities, which can be used in later life. Woodworking activities need not take up lots of space or resources if correctly planned. Ideally, a permanent area can be set up with a workbench, vice and tool storage. However, this is often not possible, so a board made of 20 mm chipboard with a rim attached underneath can be made to fit snugly over a sturdy table with a clamp-on vice. When cutting timber, it is essential that it is clamped securely for accurate results and safety. A basic tool kit should include a tape measure, ruler, try-square, tenon and panel saw, sandpaper and a number of hammers. The trick is to measure and mark out everything accurately before cutting. 'Measure twice, cut once' should be your motto. Tenon saws are easier to use and are good for everything apart from wider pieces of wood. Smaller hammers are easier than claw hammers and with them there is less of a tendency for the nails to bend. The use of tools should always be taught and supervised by an adult who is confident and experienced in their appropriate use. Make sure that when you finish an activity, tools are counted in correctly and stored in a suitable place.

Snapshot

Gina and Heava were very nervous at first of using the tools, in particular the saw as they were scared of not cutting the plywood straight down the line and making a mess of the board. With support from the youth worker, they practised holding the saw correctly and cutting along the lines they had marked on scrap pieces of board. After quite a lot of practise, they were able to cut the board accurately to size and complete the whole project. They were very proud of their finished game board and certainly gained confidence in their own abilities.

Safety Check

Use all tools in an appropriate and safe manner.
Wear rubber gloves when washing out varnish brushes

What next?

Try making other boards that you have seen—perhaps more familiar games such as drafts or try some of the others in this book. Draft pieces can be made out of old broom handles.

Feed the Birds

Why we like it

This activity encourages care for wildlife during the winter and in addition involves mixing up lots of ingredients which most people of all ages love doing. Cooking aside, it also develops observational skills and can lead onto various different projects —such as doing a bird survey of your area or other conservation related activities.

What you might need

Sturdy twigs, for example, hedge cuttings

Dry logs

Thick branches

Cooking ingredients, such as, birdseed, cooked rice, nuts, bread or cake crumbs, dried fruit, leftover cooked vegetables, porridge oats or grated cheese (about 300 g)

Suet or lard (around 100 g)

Hooks

String

Yogurt pots

Mixing bowl

Wooden spoon

Scissors

Drill and various drill bit sizes

Bowsaw (only if you need to cut logs to size)

Workbench

Safety goggles.

How many can do it

Groups of 5 or 6.

Where you can do it

A combination of in the kitchen and outside or on a safe workspace with suitable floor covering.

Snapshot

Food and water are basic necessities for all living creatures. Birds are no exception to this rule and as less wild space with trees, plants and food becomes available for them, it is good to give a helping hand. This is especially important during the frosty winter months, when berries are scarce and insects difficult to find.

How you can do it

1. Collect a selection of twigs about 20 cm long and dried logs approximately 30 cm in length and 15 cm in diameter. You can also use thick branches.

2. Secure logs firmly in a vice or workbench and drill different sized holes all the way round the log in a random pattern. Finish them off by securing a hook into one end. The best way to do this is to drill a small pilot hole before screwing in the hook.

3. Next make the bird food. You can use either a cooked or uncooked variety.

Cooked

Put a variety of the ingredients into a large bowl. Next melt the fat, in a saucepan, pour over the ingredients and stir well.

Uncooked

Leave the lard in a warm place for about an hour. Meanwhile, put some birdseed, dried fruit, peanuts (not salted) and a little grated cheese into a bowl. When the lard is soft, cut it into small pieces and add this to the ingredients. Then, and this is the fun part, using your fingertips, rub the lard evenly into the mixture. It's a bit like making pastry!

For both the above recipes, the rule of thumb is to use $^1/_4$ fat to $^3/_4$ mixture.

4. If making bird cake on twigs, pour the mixture into yogurt pots and push a stick into the middle. String can be tied to the stick to hang the bird food from a tree. Leave to set in a cool place. When mixture has cooled and set remove the yoghurt pots.

5. If you are making the feeding logs, squidge as much of the mixture into the holes in the logs as possible.

6. Hang your bird feeders from a tree or bird table and wait for the birds to arrive.

Useful Tips

The above recipes should only be used in the autumn or winter.

If the mixture is not to be used immediately, store in a fridge or else it will start to go mouldy.

If you don't have a tree or bird tables, try using hanging basket hooks, secured to the outside of your building.

Do discuss the cooking ingredients with the whole group before starting the activity as some may object to using animal fat.

Safety Check

Cooking and the use of sharp tools should be supervised by an adult.

If sawing logs to size, make sure the blade is sharp, the log is secured firmly in a vice and that the process is well supervised.

When drilling holes, again secure the logs firmly to the workbench and wear safety goggles.

If you choose to use the cooked bird food recipe, a great deal of care must be used when melting, pouring and stirring the hot fat.

Snapshot

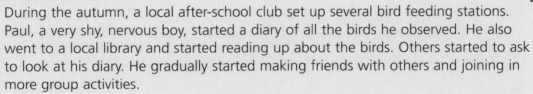

During the autumn, a local after-school club set up several bird feeding stations. Paul, a very shy, nervous boy, started a diary of all the birds he observed. He also went to a local library and started reading up about the birds. Others started to ask to look at his diary. He gradually started making friends with others and joining in more group activities.

What next?

Birds can be fed during the breeding season but be careful only to put out food that young chicks will not choke on, that is, don't use anything containing traces of peanuts or dog biscuits. Suitable food would include sultanas, black sunflower seeds, mealworms and waxworms, small pieces of apple and fine oatmeal.

The RSPB are happy to provide a wide range of leaflets and fact sheets which contain lots of information relating to birds and activities which will encourage them into your environment. Contact them at the following address, The RSPB, UK Headquarters, The Lodge, Sandy, Bedfordshire SG19 2DL or at *www.rspb.org.uk/youth*

Bird feeders can also be hung from sky hooks (see page 67).

Growing Beans

Why we like it

This is a project that lasts for months. It gives those without a garden a chance to take part in growing their own food and the beans are delicious to eat.

What you might need

Long sticks

String

A packet of runner bean seeds

Compost

A pot (optional, but if you would like to use a pot see page 43 for a cheap way of making one)

A trowel

A pair of scissors

Small stones for drainage.

How many can do it

As many people as you have materials and space for.

Where you can do it

Outside if possible but inside on a table covered in newspaper is fine.

Snapshot

Growing anything from seed, and watching it develop, can often be a learning experience for all—a time when questions are raised and a time for discussion. Many seeds need special growing conditions, such as, type of soil, heat or lack of it, specific watering schedules, special care, etc. However many settings are not geared for this kind of care for plants and have a limited amount of time and space to produce results that will keep young people interested. The following activity has been developed with these needs in mind. For those that become interested, it will give them a taster of what is possible.

How you can do it

1. Decide where you are going to plant the beans—are they going into a pot or straight into the ground?

2. Prepare the soil by digging over and raking or if you are going to plant in a pot, place stones for drainage at the bottom and fill with compost.

3. Place the sticks in the pot in a tipi shape and tie at the top. If you are planting in the ground either use the tipi method or create a tall tent shape with diagonal slats to tie it together.

4. Plant a bean on either side of the sticks according to the instructions on the packet. Water them immediately.

5. Water regularly and watch them grow!

6. Pick, cook and eat the beans when they are ready.

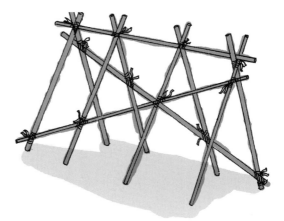

Snapshot

Fiona and her sister Gail had never grown anything before. They started off 'their' beans in small pots in April and one of the first things they did on entering the club was to check and water them. In May they planted them outside and would get really cross if someone kicked a ball near them. By the beginning of August the beans were ready to pick. They enjoyed cooking a bean feast for us all and are now keen to grow other things.

Useful Tips

Don't allow the soil to dry out but also do not over water.
As the beans grow, carefully help them to wind themselves around the sticks. When the beans are ready, pick them regularly to encourage more to grow.

Tyre Pots

Here is a cheap way to make a pot, as large pots from a garden centre or DIY store can be very expensive. It also has the added factor of you being able to make something from nothing. It is often a good idea to look at presented activities and think about how they can be successfully adapted to your own groups needs and resources. With a little thought and imagination, they may not be as difficult or expensive as you may at first think.

What you might need

Old nylon braced tyre (a steel radial tyre is impossible to cut) with hub

Chalk

Coach or hammerite paint

Brushes

Gloves

Stanley knife

Tape measure.

How many can do it

Group of four to five.

Where you can do it

Outside.

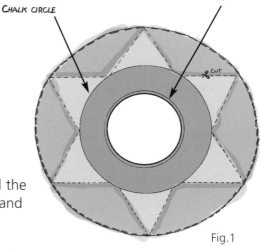

CHALK CIRCLE

RIM

CUT

Fig.1

How you can do it

1. Wash tyre.

2. Place the tyre on the floor, valve-side up and deflate by pressing in the valve with a stick until all the air is expelled. Make sure the tyre is still on its rim and if not reinflate and start again.

3. Using chalk, draw a circumfrence on the side of the tyre, 8 cm from the wheel rim. Chalk the pattern to give the shape of the pot, see Fig.1.

4. Put on thick gloves and cut carefully around the circumference using the Stanley knife. (Cut out the segments to give the pattern).

5. Turn the tyre over to enable you to pull the cut section inside out.

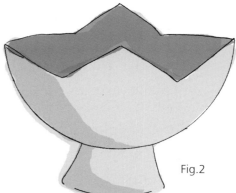

Fig.2

6. Place one foot on the hub and, putting your hands inside the cut tyre, pull upwards, peeling it inside out as you go along. At this point lots of people will need to help. (The side of the tyre that you have cut becomes the top of the pot, the middle and other side of the tyre, which you have peeled becomes the bowl. The hub is the base.) Now you're ready to decorate!

Useful Tips

Tyre shops are usually happy to give away old tyres.

The easiest tyres to use are those from a MINI.

If you cannot get hold of coach or hammerite paint, use exterior wall paint as you can always repaint the tyre as the paint wears off.

Make sure the paint is completely dry before putting in stones, compost and plants.

Safety Check

Stanley knives should be used by, or carefully supervised by, a competent adult. Make sure you work away from your body and that the area is cleared appropriately.

Old tyres are very dirty so make sure everyone is wearing old clothes or overalls.

Snapshot

A collection of old tyres had gathered in a corner near the playscheme. Although various people had been asked to take them away, this was not possible, so it was decided to turn them into something useful. The tyre pot seemed the obvious choice. As well as beans, fast growing herbs such as parsley and basil and flowers such as marigolds were grown and they provided a lovely display in the entrance as well as some good things to eat.

What next?

Try growing a variety of beans. If you've enjoyed this activity why not try growing other climbing plants such as peas, nasturtiums, sweet peas or gourds.

If you have room, make a really large tipi in the earth and grow climbing plants up it. In the summer, put rugs down and use it as a quiet space.

Think of other containers that can be used as pots, such as old saucepans with drainage holes drilled, old wheelbarrows, watering cans, pipes, etc.

Sculptures using Interesting Wooden Shapes

Why we like it

As they grow trees are subjected to many influences such as wind and rain, which make their branches twist and bend into lots of interesting shapes. This activity is based on using those natural shapes to create sculptures using branches of felled trees and it's great for getting children to use their imagination, bounce ideas off each other and work together.

What you might need

Wood from cut down trees (the more recently felled the better as your sculpture will last longer—see useful tips for ideas of where to find them)

Sawn logs

Saw

Hammer

Cordless drill

Strong gloves

Various sizes of nails

Spade and trowel

Workbench

Safety goggles

Ladder

Cloth.

Spotlight

These ideas have been inspired by the work of a community artist who works on a thriving allotment site. His allotment is dotted with amazing structures and in-between he grows a wealth of plants. Keep an eye out for community artists near you. Artists can sometimes be persuaded to come and work with your group on a joint project.

How many can do it

Groups of up to 10.

Where you can do it

Preferably outside and definitely outside for permanent sculptures. However free-standing sculptures could be made in a suitably large inside space. If you decide to do the latter make sure you protect the floor with a heavy cloth.

How you can do it

Fig.1

A permanent sculpture

Look at the wood carefully—are there any shapes that suggest an idea? Look especially at the bent shapes—do they make you think of a lip, a foot or a tongue? These will become your key pieces from which to work. What do you think you could make? Alternatively, you could already have an idea of what you would like to make and in that case look for the useful pieces and shapes to fit your design. You could make a monster, a statue, a cowboy, a fish or a bird or something completely different. The world is your oyster and you are only limited by your imagination.

All of your ideas can be made using the basic tripod method. Here is an example of how to make a figure.

1. Choose three pieces of wood, approximately the same length.

2. Dig a 60 cm deep hole and place in your main support (Fig.1).

3. Dig two other 60 cm deep holes to form a tripod. The distance from the first hole will be determined by the length of your pieces of wood.

Fig.2

4. Place in your second piece of wood and mark where it crosses the main support. Drill a small hole through the second piece and nail it in place. Repeat for the third piece (see Fig.2). Stand back and check that the structure is stable. This is the basic tripod method, which can be used for all permanent sculptures.

5. Think about the head next and find suitably shaped curvy pieces. Drill and nail in place (see Fig.3).

6. Now think about arms, wings, claws, tentacles, teeth, mouth, tongue etc. Drill and nail in place (as in Fig.4).

7. For additional strength, add more cross pieces around the base. Sometimes pieces of wood click together and start to interlock (see Fig.5). Note: if it still wobbles it is not strong enough and may fall on someone so add more base pieces digging holes to secure them. This is especially important if you are working in a very windy area!

Fig.3

8. Stand back and admire your sculpture.

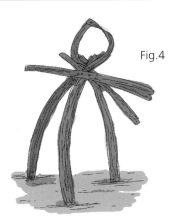
Fig.4

Fig.5

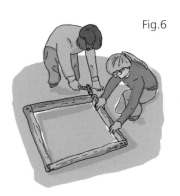
Fig.6

How you can do it

A Free-standing sculpture

These can be made to any size using the same basic structure.

1. Make a large square or triangle out of strong pieces of wood by drilling and nailing the pieces together on the ground (see Fig.6).

2. Add in three or four verticals depending on your initial base shape. Drill and nail in place (Fig.7).

3. Now look for interesting bendy pieces of wood and start to interlock and nail in place to create unusual figures and shapes (see Fig.8).

Fig.7

Fig.8

Useful Tips

Look out for cut oak as not only do you get interesting shapes but it lasts for a long time. Don't use silver birch as it rots very quickly.

Try contacting your local council to obtain materials.

This is a long term project so plan it to last over a number of weeks or months.

Think carefully about where you are going to build a permanent sculpture because you will not be able to move it once it is built.

If digging holes in the winter, you may get very muddy so wear suitable clothing and footwear.

When drilling, use a drill bit slightly smaller than the nail size.

Cross supports should be attached in two places at least.

Don't be scared to place your pieces of wood, you can always adapt your ideas.

When hammering into a wobbly support, use a block of wood behind it to keep it stable.

Your sculpture will not look the same as your diagram if you have drawn one. Don't be disappointed—go with the flow!

Safety Check

Teach and supervise correct use of tools. Note that blunt saws are more dangerous to use than sharp ones.

Always secure the piece of wood you are cutting in a vice before starting to cut.

Always carefully supervise use of saws or cordless drills (an adult may need to do the drilling).

Make sure everyone wears safety goggles and strong gloves.

Make sure that when using the ladder, it is being held securely.

When making a permanent sculpture supervise carefully the placing of the initial vertical piece and ensure that the tripod is stable enough to begin work.

What next?

Sculptures can be decorated using paint, fabric, leaves etc. or you could hang things from them, such as, beads, dreamcatchers (see page 4) or dragon's eyes (see page 1).

If you are feeling especially adventurous try making a ball. Follow these instructions:

1. Make a 3D sphere using willow (Fig.9).

2. Find pieces of wood which bend—the longer the better but short pieces will do.

3. Initially, attach pieces around the frame using string. When they start to cross over, join together using the drill and nail method (Fig.10).

4. Keep an eye on the shape but keep going until you have a completed ball (Fig.11)

Have fun inventing rolling games.

Inspiration for wooden sculptures can be found at *www.surfox.net*

Snapshot

Imagination

Curvy and twisted
Over and round
Bending and nailed
Lots more ways to be found.
Create, explore
Look and design
Think of a shape
Then make it bind.

Polly Lowe (aged 13)

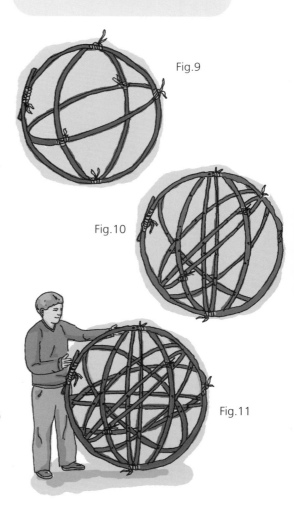

Fig.9

Fig.10

Fig.11

Search and Rescue

Why we like it

This is a great game to play on a fine day with a large group of people. It encourages working in teams and co-operative thinking, whilst at the same time improving map reading and strategy skills.

What you might need

Ten distinctive stones—perhaps use ones you have painted (see page 16) Photocopied maps and pencils.

How many can do it

As many as you like split into groups of 5 or 6.

Where you can do it

A large open space such as a park or playing field.

Safety Check

If you are playing this in a large area, each group may need supervision. Make sure you have talked to them about keeping safe whilst out and about.

Spotlight

Many parks or village greens are under-used or just thought of as a place for people to walk their dogs. However, they are great play spaces and often provide large areas for team games and activities. It is a good idea to talk about how to keep safe when out and about and what 'rules' need to be observed. The basics are:

Always stay in groups of at least two and NEVER go off on your own

Be aware of the people around you - be polite if they talk to you but don't stick around and always inform an adult if someone is making you feel uneasy

Always tell a known and trusted adult if something goes wrong. You do not have to deal with any dangerous situation or one that makes you feel uncomfortable alone.

How you can do it

1. Draw a map of the area, marking on the features, and make a copy for each group.

2. Whilst the group is inside, hide the stones in your area of play and mark their positions on your own map.

3. Give each team a map and pencil and explain that a whole team (of adventurers) has been separated and got lost. They need to be found. However, they may be injured and should not be moved. The object is to find, locate and mark on the map and report to base.

4. Start each team off in the middle of the park or field and send them off in different directions.

5. At the end of the specified time, for example, thirty minutes, collect in all the maps and check them against the original. The winning team is the one with the most stones marked correctly on their map.

Snapshot

This activity was enjoyed so much by one playscheme, that one team decided to organise the next game themselves and try it out in another nearby open space. They elected a group leader and accomplice who made the initial map and hid the stones. Later, other teams, were asked to try it out. They ended with a discussion on map drawing skills and hunting strategies, and the game continued over many days.

What next?

You could try this for an Easter egg hunt, using 'pretend eggs' with chocolate ones as prizes at the end.

Useful Tips

It's a good idea for each team to choose a name for itself and write this on their map.

Establish any rules before they set off, such as, stay in your group and the allocated area, no talking to other groups and above all do not move the stones.

Check that someone in the team is wearing a watch.

Trail Laying

Why we like it

Most of us enjoyed playing hide and seek when we were younger and this is a great activity for large groups of independent young people and adults. It uses no equipment and minimal materials.

What you might need

A large supply of sticks and stones.

How many can do it

As many as you like.

Where you can do it

Outside in a large area with plenty of places to hide. The best place is in a woodland.

Spotlight

There are certain countryside rules that should be observed when out and about. These rules are not to stop us having fun but to safeguard the countryside and ourselves:

Take all litter home

Look after wildlife, plants and trees

Never start a fire unless you have permission to do so in a designated area

Keep to public paths across farmland and if uncertain check the path is open and safe to use

Use gates and stiles to cross fences, hedges and walls

Close all gates behind you

Leave farm animals, machinery and crops alone

Keep water clean and unpolluted.

How you can do it

1. Split into two teams and decide which team will hide first and how long the second team has to wait before they follow them.

2. Team A goes off, laying a trail of stick arrows, showing their path. They can also lay false trails. At the end of a false trail a pile of stones is left to indicate to the tracking Team B that they have gone the wrong way.

3. When Team A feel they have laid a long enough trail, they find a good hiding place and try to keep quiet.

4. After the agreed waiting time, Team B tracks them down.

5. Once Team A has been found the two teams swap roles.

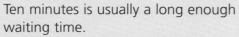

Useful Tips

Ten minutes is usually a long enough waiting time.

It's advisable to play another game (see *Serious Fun: Games for 10–14s* in the Can Do series) whilst the tracking group is waiting.

Both groups need to be careful not to disturb the trail once it's been laid, for obvious reasons.

It's important to stress that this is different from hide and seek, in that the object is for the hiding group to lay a good enough trail for the tracking group to find it.

Safety Check

Since this activity will take place in the country, it's essential to follow the Countryside Code.

It is also important that no team member gets lost and that teams look after each other. Arrange a rendezvous point in advance.

Make sure that a number of team members are wearing a watch.

Snapshot

One group experimented by having two trail lying teams and two following teams. Teams were allowed to ambush the following team, if they discovered they had followed the wrong team. It was great fun for most but did create a lot of noise and some team members did not enjoy being taken prisoner or the interruption to their own tracking activity.

What next?

Try laying trails using other materials such as flour, acorns, conkers, etc.

Travelling Sticks

Why we like it

This is an activity that can be done at any time of the year and in most types of weather providing that everyone is kitted out correctly. Each time a journey is taken different results are produced, feelings expressed and friendships formed.

What you might need

A stick for each person about 60cms long (keep an eye out for someone cutting a hedge)

Balls of string or wool

Sticky tape

Scissors.

How many can do it

Large group split into small groups.

Where you can do it

Outside.

Spotlight

We all journey from one place to another on a continual basis, seeing, smelling, hearing, tasting and feeling the world around us. The walk to school, the summer or winter holiday, a coach trip or cycle ride, all give us new sights, smells, sounds, tastes and textures to store in our memory bank. Some of us depend more on one sense than on others; some of us do not have or have lost the use of one or more senses but use what we have to the best of our abilities. But all of us need time to reflect and share our experiences with others. This activity gives everyone a good excuse to go for a walk and then time to talk about it. It is surprising how the same journey can be perceived in so many different ways.

How you can do it

1. Each person should choose a stick while you introduce the concept of walking and collecting so that a history of individual adventures will be able to be told by each member or group. For example, a leaf collected can indicate that the individual started their journey near a clump of trees where she spent time looking at the autumn colours; a duck's feather may indicate that the individual walked past a small pond where they watched a mother with her ducklings; a piece of lavender could show that the individual walked past a lavender hedge and enjoyed the smell of it, and so on.

2. Everyone needs to understand a few basic rules, for example, no one is to pick up dangerous or precious items or plants. This will vary depending on whether the walk is to take place in the city, park or woodlands. You will have your own local environment to consider and your own advice to give. Agree a completion time and a rendezvous point.

3. Send each group, in a different direction. This means that not only will each individual have their own story to tell but there will also be a collective group story.

4. Make sure that you allow time during the walk for the group to sit down and tie the collected items onto the stick by wrapping the string or wool round them. Large items can be attached using sticky tape but this does not create such a good visual effect.

5. At the end of the walk, find somewhere comfortable to sit and let individuals or groups share their travelling story with each other.

6. Display the sticks by hanging them up together or sticking them in a pattern in the ground.

Useful Tips

In groups, have lots of small balls of wool or string rather than several larger ones as this means that everyone can tie their collected items on at the same time and not get on top of one another.

Leave the base of the stick bare if you want to finally stick them into the ground.

Safety Check

As mentioned above do stress items that are able to be collected and those that are definitely not to be touched. Find time to walk around the area to check, prior to the walk taking place.

Take time to sit and tie your items onto your stick during the walk, as this will mean that no-one will accidentally trip with scissors in their hands and that little pieces of wool do not get scattered and left all over the your walk area.

Snapshot

An after-school club set in an inner city area decided to visit a nearby nature park which was rarely used by the young people they worked with. At first there was some degree of reluctance about 'going on a walk' but as the group had recently made a sky hook (see page 67), they were persuaded that travelling sticks would decorate the hook beautifully and allow them a chance to make their own unique statement on it. Many of the sticks were finished with bits of plants, the odd bone, some unusual shaped stones, etc. Shane presented a stick with lots of sweet wrappers, crisp packets and drinks cans tied to it. When asked to tell his story, he explained that when he was told he was going to a nature reserve, he expected to see lots of nice things and that instead he had found lots of litter. His stick told the story of the walk through the litter he had found, for example, the drink cans had been found under the bench by the pond, the sweet wrappers near a conker tree, etc. The afterschool club later asked a member from the voluntary nature reserve group to come and speak to them, which subsequently led to tree planting activities, a litter blitz, creating a seasonal photographic record of the area and helping to build new paths.

What next?

Introduce the idea of using the colours of the wool to reflect the things that you have seen in your environment, for example, a walk across a grassy meadow on a beautiful sunny day can be shown by grass being tied onto the stick using sky blue wool. Additionally, items collected can be tied to make shapes of things that have been seen on the journey, such as, feathers in the shape of a bird, conkers on a branch to show a large horse chestnut tree, etc.

Building Dens

Why we like it

This is a great group activity that requires planning, loads of discussion, problem solving and results in a semi-permanent play resource that is almost like building an extension on to your setting.

What you might need

Newly cut hazel poles—as straight as possible and at least 2 m long by 2–3 cm thick in diameter. The number will depend on the size and shape of the bender you are planning to build.

Tarpaulins or groundsheets (plastic or canvas) if you wish your den to be rain proof)

Old sheets or blankets

String

Scissors

Bow saw

Long metal spike for making holes

Lump hammer

Eyelet kit (optional see Useful Tips on page 59).

How many can do it

A group of 8.

Where you can do it

Most likely outside—chose your spot carefully if making a permanent structure—but small moveable benders can be made inside.

Spotlight

Benders and tipis have been built by many travelling people over the last couple of centuries and more. They are built, by their owners, to provide both temporary and permanent homes. In the play setting they provide, in their simple form, good dens, a quiet area to escape the crowd and some shade in which to shelter from the hot sun, wind or rain.

Building a Bender

How you can do it

A permanent structure

1. Design your bender on paper first. Is it going to be dome or tunnel shaped? How many upright and cross poles will you require?

2. Mark out the chosen area with pegs and string.

3. Using the metal spike and mallet, make holes 20–30 cm deep to put the upright poles in.

4. Place each upright into position before bending opposite poles together to make an arch.

5. Tie them securely together.

6. Now weave the crosspieces around the uprights until the whole structure feels secure. Make sure you plan where the door is going to be.

7. If the structure still feels shaky, lash the crosspieces to the uprights as shown below.

8. Cover with tarpaulin or old sheets or blankets depending on how permanent and weather proof you want the bender to be. Tie them into position.

9. Lay your groundsheet or blankets on the ground.

10. Your bender is ready to move into.

How you can do it

A moveable structure

Follow the instructions above except you must lash the uprights to the crosspieces, including horizontal base cross pieces. Before stage 8, carefully pull the uprights out of the ground and move the bender wherever you want to. As mentioned above, it is possible to make a small bender inside, but you will need lots of helpers to hold and bend the upright poles until they are securely lashed into position.

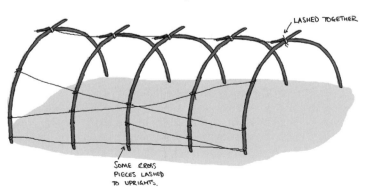

LASHED TOGETHER

SOME CROSS PIECES LASHED TO UPRIGHTS.

Building a Tipi

What you might need

Six to eight 3 m long poles (thick bamboo canes would do) although the number and length will vary depending on the how big you are planning to build you tipi. Full size habitable tipis require 12–14 poles about 7 m long and tapering from 10 cm to 3 cm in thickness!

Tarpaulins and groundsheets (only if you wish your den to be rain proof)

Old sheets or blankets

Scissors

Bow

Eyelet kit (optional)

Thin rope.

How many can do it

A group of around 8–10 people.

Where you can do it

Preferably outside but it also possible to build a temporary structure inside.

Snapshot

Benders and tipis can be used as craft areas, places to hang out, to prepare and eat picnics, imaginative play areas, quiet reading and game areas, a good place to withdraw for private conversations, as well as permanent homes and living spaces.

How you can do it

1. Design your tipi on paper first. How many uprights will you require?

2. Lay 3 poles on the ground and lash them together about 60cm from the top using at least 6 m of rope. Use enough rope to secure the poles, but leave enough spare for later use.

3. Stand the poles up as a tripod, making sure that each pole has a member of the group supporting it in position.

4. Start to lay the other poles onto the tripod. Bring the spare rope to the outside of the tipi and wind around the poles, 4 times, at the point where they cross. When the poles are secure peg the remaining rope to the ground inside the tipi, to prevent it blowing away in high winds.

5. Loop a rope around the bottom of the poles.

6. Cover with tarpaulin or old sheets or blankets depending on how permanent and weather proof you want the tipi to be. Tie them into position.

7. Lay your groundsheet or blankets on the ground.

8. Make your tipi habitable with rugs, sheepskins and cushions.

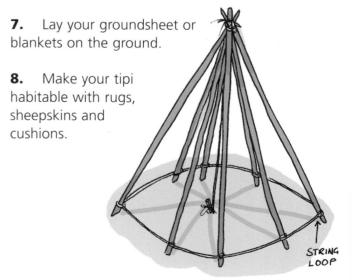

STRING LOOP

Spotlight

Tipis were used as homes by the nomadic North American Indians for centuries. They were easy to erect and dismantle and were transported on a structure called a travois (which was made and owned by women) drawn by a horse. The cover was traditionally made from buffalo hide and only later canvas was used. Once erected, a traditional tipi would have a central fire burning for warmth and cooking.

Useful Tips

If the tipi is to be situated inside, tie string between the bottom of the poles in a loop, otherwise they sink gracefully to the floor and refuse to stay up.

You shouldn't need a step ladder but it is handy to have one, as you may need it when tying the top of the poles.

Cloth and tarpaulin can be more securely fastened into position if eyelets are made.

Eyelet kits make non-tearing holes in fabric. They can be obtained from upholsterers.

Tipis and benders covered in dyed muslin make magical spaces.

Safety Check

Use the lump hammer and the metal spike in a responsible manner.

Make sure you have enough helpers to hold the poles before starting these projects.

To mark out a perfect circle tie a piece of string to the top of a stick, fix it in the ground, tie the other end of the string to another stick at half the diameter you require and walk round placing pegs or marking the earth as you go.

What next?

You could have a go at making miniature tipi or bender villages using twigs and small pieces of scrap material. If you want to find out more about tipis, try looking at *http://www.tipis-tepees-tepees.com* on the web.

A fantastic book for information on the history, construction and use of tipis is *The Indian Tipi*, by Reginald and Gladys Laubin, published by University of Oaklahoma Press, 1977.

Fire Building

Why we like it

Most people love a fire and the smell of wood smoke. Fires become a communal gathering place, a place to sit and relax, to cook food, share stories or play music and sing. There are many ways to make a fire and listed below are just a few and a selection of materials you can use.

What you might need

Tinder: Seed-heads of Rosebay willow herb or clematis, dead bracken, dried bark from honeysuckle, birch, cherry or cedar trees, dry grass or cotton grass, punk (the dried rotten remains of wood) —or newspaper will do.

Kindling—various sizes of dry wooden sticks and twigs placed in graded piles: matchstick thin, thicker than a match but thinner than a pencil, pencil thickness

Small fuel—thicker than a pencil but not as thick as your thumb

Large fuel—branches that you can easily break over your knee

Logs—these are only needed on large fires, which are going to burn for several hours

Matches

Tongs.

How many can do it

Everyone can join in collecting fuel but a fire needs to be lit in a controlled manner by only a small group of people.

Where you can do it

Outside, preferably in a designated permanent fireplace. Alternatively you can use a spare patch of bare earth or cut a large turf from the grass and put to one side to replace after the fire is finished. Make sure the fire is positioned away from low hanging tree branches, bushes or buildings. If you prefer not to have an open fire that marks the ground, you can light the fire in an old metal wheel hub or an old washing machine drum with holes drilled in the bottom with a wire mesh to stop small fuel falling out the bottom. Position this firmly on bricks to raise it off the ground. Make sure there is enough clear space around the fire for people to sit. You can use sticks or logs to mark a circle around the fire place indicating the area which must not be entered whilst the fire is alight.

How you can do it

1. If lighting a fire on bare earth, use small fuel to build a platform about 40 cm square to raise the fire off damp ground.

2. Place a large ball of tinder on the platform and some handfuls of fine kindling in a wig-wam shape over it.

3. Light the tinder and, as the fire burns, gradually add more kindling of increasing size.

4. By now the fire should be burning nicely so add increasingly larger fuel.

5. Continue to feed the fire as you sit back to enjoy it.

Spotlight

Good fire building takes time, preparation and some know-how. Fire provides places for us to cook, have lighting, meet and keep warm. Fire is a vital element within all human societies, but it is one that needs to be controlled and used appropriately at all times. Fire always has the potential to be dangerous, and for this reason many playsettings in this country have stopped using open fires and naked flames such as candles. However we have found that it is usually those children who have no experience of fire who are most likely to use it in a dangerous manner. It is important therefore that young people are given opportunities to learn about the properties of fire at first hand—both how to use it positively and responsibly and how to respond to its potential hazards. A permanent open fire place, if possible, can be a tremendous asset to any setting—as a place of warmth on a cold day, as a life-skill learning opportunity and a place for social gatherings. Fires need constant supervision.

Useful Tips

Tinder must be bone dry in order to light. If using newspaper, tear into strips and roll round your hand to make a ball. This prevents the paper flying off when it is lit.

When collecting fuel, look for dead wood caught in branches off the ground as these will be drier and will burn better with less smoke.

If the fire starts to fail, don't just pile more kindling on top of larger fuel as this will not help. Remove the larger fuel with tongs and get the heart of the fire going again.

Don't get disheartened if your fire doesn't light first time, just keep trying. It takes years of practise to become a skilful fire maker.

Safety Check

Safety with fire and around fire is a major consideration.

NEVER start a fire in an unpermitted area or where there is a risk of fire spreading into dry grass, bushes, trees or buildings of any kind.

Control your fire by confining it to a specific area. Build and feed it carefully, never allowing it to burn too high.

Make sure that everyone is sitting at a safe distance from the fire as sparks do fly and occasionally fuel will fall. Keep a pair of tongs handy for these occasions.

Never leave a fire burning unsupervised, even for a short while.

Keep a bucket of water or sand handy, in case of emergencies.

If using a wheel hub or washing machine drum, remember that the metal will get very hot and remain hot for some time after the fire has gone out.

Always clear up completely after a fire—make sure there are no sparks still burning, that the ground is swept clear of ash, unused wood is piled neatly and that leaves are scattered on bare earth or the turf replaced. The aim is to leave no trace of the fire at all.

Snapshot

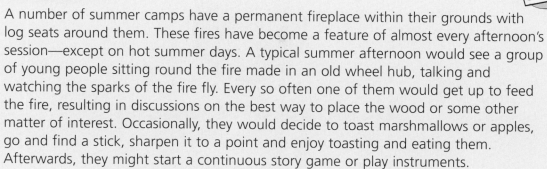

A number of summer camps have a permanent fireplace within their grounds with log seats around them. These fires have become a feature of almost every afternoon's session—except on hot summer days. A typical summer afternoon would see a group of young people sitting round the fire made in an old wheel hub, talking and watching the sparks of the fire fly. Every so often one of them would get up to feed the fire, resulting in discussions on the best way to place the wood or some other matter of interest. Occasionally, they would decide to toast marshmallows or apples, go and find a stick, sharpen it to a point and enjoy toasting and eating them. Afterwards, they might start a continuous story game or play instruments.

What next?

You could investigate ancient fire lighting techniques such as fire by friction or fire from flint sparks and have a go yourselves.

Cooking with Sticks

Why we like it

Most people want to join in and do something that they can't normally do in every day life. Cooking with sticks is fun and quick and, as long as it's well supervised, provides a lovely activity around the fire. This activity follows the fire building activity on page 60.

What you might need

Flour (self-raising flour works best)

Water

Your choice of optional fillings, such as, jam, honey, chocolate spread, lemon and sugar, cooked vegetarian or meat sausages and ketchup, marshmallows, etc.

Long sharp sticks

Bowl

Wooden spoon.

Spotlight

Cooking food over a fire provides a memory and a taste that lasts a lifetime. Many people consider this to be a complicated and time consuming activity, requiring lots of time, preparation and special equipment. However the activities suggested below need a minimal amount of materials.

How many can do it

A small group at a time.

Where you can do it

Around a fire.

How you can do it

1. Sharpen the end of your stick to a point (see Whittling Sticks on page 71).

2. Make dough by tipping flour into a bowl and gradually adding water to make a firm but not sticky consistency.

3. Take a small ball of dough each and roll it into a sausage shape using your hands.

4. Wind the dough round the stick and gently press it in place to hold it secure.

5. Now toast it over the fire, turning it continuously until it is cooked.

6. Remove the dough twist from the stick and eat straight away with your preferred filling, such as, a cooked sausage or a spoonful of jam. A squeeze of lemon juice and rolled in sugar makes your dough twist taste very much like a pancake.

7. Finish your snack with toasted marshmallows.

Useful Tips

Do blow on the marshmallow and be cautious when eating. They taste delicious but can burn your tongue or lips if you're not careful!

If possible use green (that is, newly cut) sticks, as these will have less of a chance of catching fire.

Safety Check

Use the knife carefully to sharpen the sticks (see Whittling Sticks, on page 71) and pack away safely.

Have clean tea towels ready to hold hot cooked items.

Keep a bucket and glass of water handy. Minor burns are best treated by immediately immersing in cold water for several minutes.

Never leave a fire activity or a fire unsupervised.

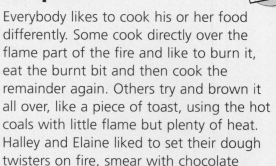

Snapshot

Everybody likes to cook his or her food differently. Some cook directly over the flame part of the fire and like to burn it, eat the burnt bit and then cook the remainder again. Others try and brown it all over, like a piece of toast, using the hot coals with little flame but plenty of heat. Halley and Elaine liked to set their dough twisters on fire, smear with chocolate spread when half cooked, cook some more and then cut into little bits which they would then eat piping hot.

What next?

Try experimenting with other food on sticks, such as, pieces of apple, muffins, bread, etc. You may find a forked stick works better in some cases.

For a more filling meal, try wrapping small potatoes in tinfoil and cooking in the embers of the fire. Another great favourite is to take a banana with its skin on, make a slit down one side, stuff with chocolate, wrap with foil and again cook in the embers of the fire. It makes a deliciously gooey desert.

A dough twister

Sky Hooks

Why we like it

This activity encourages a wide range of skills such as the use of tools, rope lashing, creativity and art. It can be done with a mixed age and ability group and creates a spectacular result in a relatively short amount of time. Sky hooks are best used in the dark, so this is a great autumn and winter activity.

What you might need

2 long straight pieces of timber around 2½–3 m tall and about 15–30 cm in diameter

One long straight piece of timber between 5–6½ m (to make the hook) 15–30 cm in diameter

One piece of timber about 2–3 m long

(If you know of anyone chopping down a Leilandi tree, this makes ideal material!)

3 hula hoops (or willow or hazel straight lengths which can be woven into large circles using the same method as for dreamcatchers, see page 4)

Thin rope and wooden stakes or sturdy tent pegs

Glass jars, such as jam jars

Thin wire

Candles

Glass paint and small paint brushes

Saw

Wire cutters

Metal spike

Step ladder

Spades

Lump hammer

Tin opener

Drill and drill bits

Safety goggles

Tin cans, drink cans.

How many can do it

Small or large groups—up to 20.

Where you can do it

Outside on an earth or grass area.

How you can do it

1. Lay the two long pieces and the shorter piece in an 'A' shape on the ground and 'lash' securely together (see Building a Bender, page 57). Make sure a good sized cleft is allowed at the apex (see Fig.1).

2. Position the 'A' frame, ensuring that enough space is left in front and behind. Mark where the frame is to sit in the ground and using the metal spike and spades, dig two holes and secure frame at an angle in ground. Knock in two wooden stakes and lash to 'A' frame for extra security.

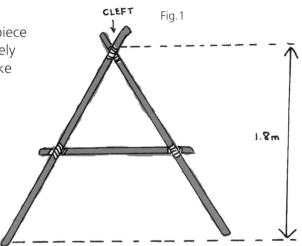

CLEFT   Fig.1

1.8m

3. Now make the sky hook by attaching rope to the end of the sky hook timber and hanging the hoops off it, one under the other, leaving at least 30 cm between each hoop.

4. Place the sky hook in the cleft of the apex then stake and lash to the ground securely. This means the hook can be lowered and raised as necessary.

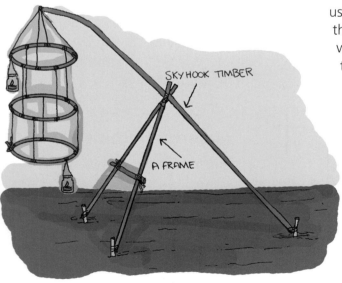

SKY HOOK TIMBER

A FRAME

Fig.2

5. The sky hook can now be decorated using glass jars with night-lights in them. Hang these off the hoops by winding thin gardener's wire round the top of the jars and creating a loop over the hoops (see Fig.2). You may need a stepladder to reach the top of the hook.

6. For an even more spectacular result, paint the jars using glass paints in designs of your choosing.

Spotlight

All play opportunities in this book can, of course, use new materials bought from the shops, timber merchant or your local DIY store. However one of the joys in creating interesting structures, games and craft activities is to use recycled materials found in your local environment. These are often bits and pieces that can be salvaged, cleaned up and reused. The trick is to keep your eyes open and think creatively. The other tip is to think about the businesses and traders around you, what they produce and sell and most importantly what they throw away, for example, wrongly mixed paint, lengths of material or carpet, scraps of wood, end of lines, etc. Often if approached, you will find they are more than happy to help. This way, you can do more, and less waste is produced. Sometimes you may have an activity in mind and be on the look out for certain materials, in which case you need to think about storage and durability. In other cases, you may well spot materials that the next day can be turned into something creative, practical or magical.

Useful Tips

Make sure the glass jars are clean and dry to maximise the light given from the candles.

Permanent markers or felt pens can be used instead of glass paint.

When stringing the hoops up, use four pieces of thin rope per hoop, the first hoop hangs like a chandelier, the others hang directly off it.

Sky hooks can be made smaller or larger depending on their final purpose—just scale the above measurements up or down to suit.

Safety Check

Store and use tools in an appropriate manner. This way nothing gets lost and nobody gets hurt.

When using the ladder to hang the glass jars, make sure it is balanced firmly on the ground and that whilst one person is up the ladder, someone else is holding it steady. The person on the ladder should never over-stretch himself as this may cause them to overbalance and fall.

Light the night lights before dropping them into the glass jars (the smaller the jar, the easier this is) or use a long wax candle-lighting taper. Never try to light a night light when it is in the jar with a match or a lighter, as you will almost certainly burn yourself.

Snapshot

At a summer camp in Wales, a group, including some with physical and learning special needs, made and decorated a sky hook over a number of days. On the last evening a concert was planned and the sky hook was used in the centre for illumination, with additional candles in jars to mark out the stage area. It was a really magical evening.

What next?

Sky hooks can be decorated in lots of ways. They can be painted with interesting patterns, have dreamcatchers or dragon eyes or some simple lanterns hung from them.

To make a drink can lantern

1. Cut the top off a clean washed drink can using a tin opener.

2. Then using a Stanley knife cut slits down the sides of the can. (The use of Stanley knives should always be undertaken or closely supervised by an adult.) When using the knife, always work away from your body and downwards. This will ensure that you do not cut yourself. These are potentially dangerous tools to work with and should only be used by a skilled practitioner—if used incorrectly they can result in very deep cuts.

3. Now gently squash the can so that the middle of each section points outward to form a 'Chinese' lantern shape.

4. The lantern is now ready to paint.

To make a tin lantern

1. Take a clean dry empty tin (catering size coffee tins work well) with the lid cut off and clamp it into a vice securely.

2. Using a metal drill bit, drill holes all round the tin either in a set pattern or randomly. Using different sized drill bits can create varying effects.

3. Finish by decorating the outside of your lantern.

Safety Check

Wear protective eye goggles when drilling and gloves when painting, to protect you from sharp edges.

Useful Tips

When making holes in cans find a log to fill the inside of the can, before drilling, to prevent the can getting squashed or bent.

Whittling Sticks

Why we like it

This is a very absorbing and satisfying activity requiring concentration and patience. It helps to develop skills in using a potentially dangerous tool. Whittling can become a cheap and creative hobby for many people. With a little practice, 'green ' or soft woods are easy to cut into a wide variety of shapes and patterns.

What you might need

Squares of leather or thick sacking which are big enough to cover your lap

Straight hazel branches—about 100 cm long and 3 cm in diameter

A selection of small sharp knives with safety catches and a good grip.

A bow saw.

How many can do it

Groups of 4 to 8, depending on how confident you feel.

Where you can do it

Outside in a quiet area, away from ball or running games.

Safety Check

Never use blunt knives as they will lead to frustration and are far more dangerous than sharp knives. Sharp knives slice the green wood accurately whereas people tend to hack with a blunt knife, which can result in accidents.

Always hold the stick upright and work away from the body. NEVER cut upwards, that is, towards the holding hand.

When getting up or walking around, the knife must be snapped shut and left on the square of leather or sacking.

If you go on to play Pooh sticks, take all the precautions needed for any waterside play and be aware that it's not good to hang too far over bridges.

Snapshot

A group of 10–14 years olds sat together whittling. Each was totally absorbed in the task and very little chatting was heard. Sam completely stripped the bark off and showed the others how smooth her stick felt. Marie created lots of tiny stripes all the way down the stick—hers was a magic wand. Faj cut large bands with some zig-zag details—his was a Martial Arts staff with protective powers.

How you can do it

1. Make sure you know how to use and hold a knife correctly and safely. Always point the blade away from your body and cut in a direction away from your body.

2. Cover your lap with leather or sacking to protect your knees.

3. There are many types of patterns that can be created on the walking sticks. In order to create stripes, cut around the branch twice and then, working down, with the stick upright, carefully cut the bark away. Zigzags are more complicated but can be achieved by scoring the wood as for stripes, and then cutting downward 'V' shapes.

What next?

As your group becomes more skilful, they may want to try writing their initials or name on the stick. Use the same method as creating the stripes but be aware of curved cuts, enthusiasm may result in you forgetting the health and safety rules about how to use a knife correctly.

If you have a river or a stream with a bridge nearby, why not have a go at whittling shorter sticks and using them to play pooh sticks?

Useful Tips

If felling hazel, always cut sticks on a slant away from the heart of the clump. This means that rain will fall away from the tree and not rot the stump.

The whittler should sit comfortably, either on a stable rock or log or with their back to a tree.

When you have reached half way down your stick, turn it round and work on the other half.

Always thoroughly clean and dry knives after use to prevent rusting. Also make sure they are sharpened before using again.

Contact your nearest council to discuss access to woodlands or wood. They may even know of someone skilled at hazel coppicing who will help organise this activity with you.

Squares of old leather can sometimes be got from upholsterers repairing chairs. Sacking can be got from rice and sugar suppliers or garden centres.

Spotlight

At Wittenham Clumps in South Oxfordshire, the World Pooh-Stick Championships have taken place for the last fourteen years. Teams of six, many in fancy dress, drop different coloured sticks from each of the two bridges at the lock. It is a great fun day out for families and their teddy bears and raises money every year for the Royal National Lifeboat Institution. It is played by dropping your stick into the main river flow and running to the other side to see where your stick is. If it comes out first, you are the winner. If you're not you have another go. When people get serious with this game, and they do, tie different coloured ribbons or wool to their sticks and appoint a referee, so that there is no argument.